Cat

My First

BGTB

Please return / renew this item by the last date shown above
Dychwelwch / Adnewyddwch erbyn y dyddiad olaf y nodir yma

Clothes

skirt

pyjamas

shoes

coat

Clothes

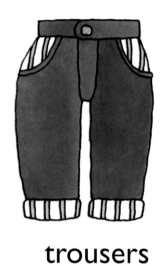

trousers

dress

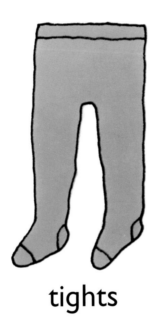

tights

hat

Clothes

T-shirt

boots

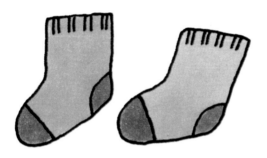

socks

swimming costume

ball

crayons

doll

drum

blocks

tricycle

teddy bear

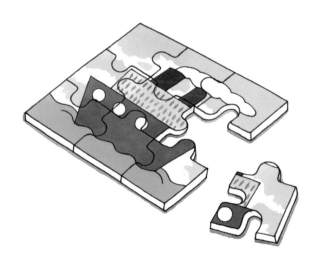

puzzle

Food

apple

bread

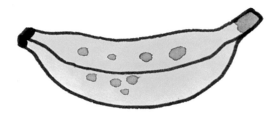

banana

egg

cheese

carrot

chocolate

water

tomato

pasta

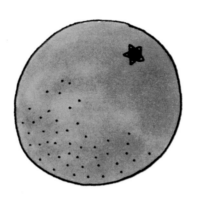

orange

sandwich

biscuits

cake

drink

balloon

Party

party hat

present

ice-cream

cupcakes

Bathtime

towel

shampoo

toothbrush

soap

Cooking

spoon

saucepan

bowl

apron

Playground

sandpit

swing

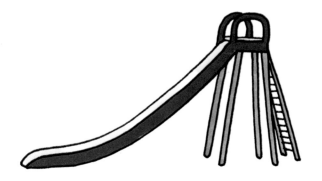

slide

bench

cat

dog

bird

mouse

cow

goat

rabbit

sheep

chicken

horse

pig

duck

Transport

car

boat

aeroplane

motorbike

Transport

bicycle

bus

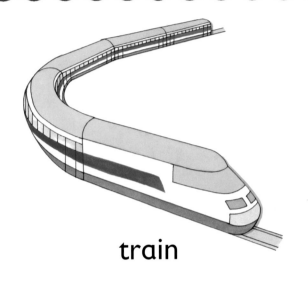

train

tractor

Weather

cloud

rain

umbrella

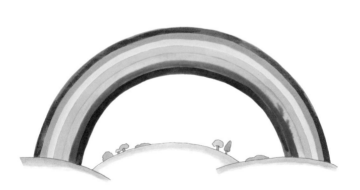

rainbow

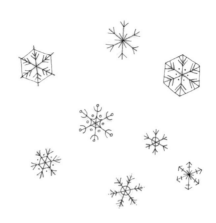

snow

storm

snowman

sun

Colours

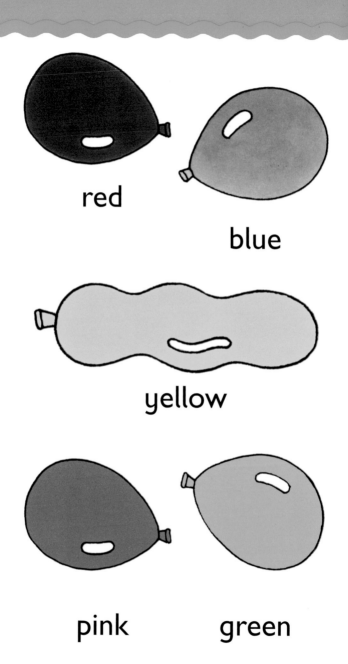

red

blue

yellow

pink   green

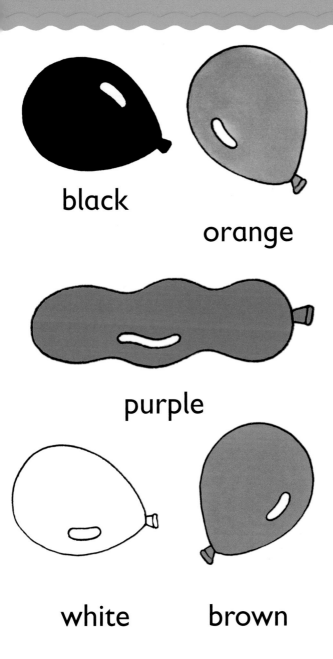

black

orange

purple

white   brown

Numbers

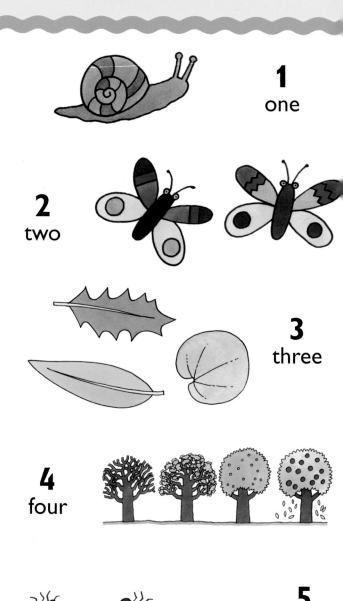

1 one

2 two

3 three

4 four

5 five

6
six

7
seven

8
eight

9
nine

10
ten

45

Word list

aeroplane
animals
apple
apron
ball
balloon
banana
bathtime
bench
bicycle
bird
biscuits
black
blocks
blue
boat
boots
bowl
bread

brown
bus
cake
car
carrot
cat
cheese
chicken
chocolate
clothes
cloud
coat
colours
cooking
cow
crayons
cupcakes
dog
doll

dress
drink
drum
duck
egg
eight
five
food
four
goat
green
hat
horse
ice-cream
motorbike
mouse
nine
numbers
one

orange (colour)

orange (fruit)

party

party hat

pasta

pig

pink

playground

present

purple

puzzle

pyjamas

rabbit

rain

rainbow

red

sandpit

sandwich

saucepan

seven

shampoo

sheep

shoes

six

skirt

slide

snow

snowman

soap

socks

spoon

storm

sun

swimming costume

swing

teddy bear

ten

three

tights

tomato

toothbrush

towel

toys

tractor

train

transport

tricycle

trousers

T-shirt

two

umbrella

water

weather

white

yellow

© b small publishing ltd. 2012

The Book Shed, 36 Leyborne Park, Kew,
Richmond, Surrey, TW9 3HA

www.bsmall.co.uk

www.facebook.co.uk/bsmallpublishing

www.twitter.com/bsmallbear

ISBN: 978-1-908164-22-3

1 2 3 4 5

Editorial: Catherine Bruzzone and Louise Millar

Design: Louise Millar

Production: Madeleine Ehm

Printed in China by WKT Co. Ltd.

British Library Cataloguing-in-Publication Data.
A catalogue record for this book
is available from the British Library.